Legal Self-Help - Save A Bundle

By Don Alexander (2012)

All Rights Reserved

Represent yourself when you need:

An Uncontested Divorce
A Living Will
A Power of Attorney
A Last Will and Testament
To File Chapter 7 Bankruptcy
To File A Small Claim
To Legally Change Your Name

Relevant Forms And Instructions

Chapters

1. Filing Chapter 7 Bankruptcy
2. Filing An Uncontested Divorce
3. Composing A Living Will
4. Composing A Power Of Attorney
5. Composing A Last Will And Testament
6. Filing A Small Claim
7. Filing For A Legal name Change

Disclaimer:

This book is intended to supply information for those individuals who wish to represent themselves without the expense of an attorney and in no instance is to be construed as legal advice pursuant to paid representation by a practicing attorney.

Chapter One
Filing Chapter 7 Bankruptcy

FILING CHAPTER 7 PERSONAL BANKRUPTCY INFORMATION PACKET AND FORMS INSTRUCTIONS

General Information

Personal bankruptcy petitions are filed, heard and decided in our federal court system within specific federal bankruptcy courts. There is a designated federal bankruptcy court in every federal judicial circuit. To determine the location of the bankruptcy court for the county in which you reside, look in your local telephone yellow pages under United States Government, Bankruptcy Court; or enter United States Bankruptcy Court for your county of residence in the internet search bar and click on the "search" or "go" link.

Chapter 7 Bankruptcy allows a debtor whose financial obligations exceed his/her assets and income to discharge both secured and unsecured debts in order to "get a fresh start." However, there are some sacrifices and downside considerations that should be carefully considered prior to filing a Chapter 7 Bankruptcy. There are other options for partial debt liquidation under other Bankruptcy Chapters about which volumes have been written. For any bankruptcy filing other than Chapter 7, it is best to be represented by an attorney who specializes in bankruptcy proceedings.

A Chapter 7 bankruptcy is simple and quite easy to obtain if one is willing to give up all non-exempt personal assets and to endure a bad credit rating for eight to ten years. A debtor seeking a Chapter 7 debt discharge must provide the bankruptcy court clerk with a Credit Counseling Certificate pursuant to credit counseling by a provider approved by the court as listed at www.usdoj.gov/ust or by calling an informational number provided by the court clerk. The credit counselor provides the certificate which is then filed with the court by debtor. There is no form involved. Subject to limited exceptions, a debtor must complete an instructional course in personal financial management before receiving a discharge under Chapter 7. Debtor must also complete and file a "Debtor's Certificate of Completion of Instructional Course Concerning Personal Financial Management" using the official Chapter 7 Bankruptcy form. This certificate must be filed before a discharge can be officially entered. This certificate must be filed within 45 days after the first date set for the meeting of creditors. Failure to timely file this certificate could result in debtor's case being closed without a court order discharging debts and there is a reopening fee of $260.00. For a list of approved providers of this required instructional course go to the website www.usdoj.gov/ust or call the local federal bankruptcy court clerk.

Exempt personal assets are determined by federal law and state law which varies widely from state to state. Thus, personal assets exempt from creditors will usually be determined by the state where the debtor has resided for a statutory period. The state residency requirement for a specified period of time, in order to take advantage of asset exemptions under state law, is intended to keep debtors from moving temporarily to a state with more favorable exemption just prior to filing a Chapter 7 bankruptcy and then moving back to a state allowing less favorable exemptions. Furthermore, state law will specify whether a debtor may claim only state exemptions or choose between federal or state exemptions. In some states, the debtor may be able to claim state exemptions and a very limited number of specific federal exemptions not exempted under state law.

Consequently, a debtor considering a Chapter 7 Bankruptcy should immediately obtain a list of state allowed exemptions from the internet or public library. Use this search phrase: "(name of your state) exemptions under Chapter 7 Bankruptcy."

The state you must use is the state you lived in for the 730 days (2 years) before filing; or if you did not live in a single state in the previous two years you use the state where you lived the majority of the 180 day period preceding the 2 year period; or if the preceding state residency requirement renders you ineligible for any state exemptions then the debtor is allowed to choose the federal exemptions. A list of federal exemptions can also be obtained from the internet or public library using the search phrase: "federal exemptions under Chapter 7 bankruptcy."

To appreciate how important state allowed exemptions are, consider the following examples.

Note: Each separate exemption includes a reference to the statutory authority for the exemption:

Missouri exemptions

MISSOURI STATE EXEMPTION STATUTES --- FEDERAL BANKRUPTCY EXEMPTIONS ARE NOT AVAILABLE.

All law references are to Annotated Missouri Statutes unless otherwise noted.

**ASSET EXEMPTION LAW PROVISION
Homestead Real property to $8000 or mobile home to $1000 (joint owners may not double)**

Property held as tenancy for the entirety may be exempt against debts owed by only one spouse 513.430(6), 513.475, *In re Anderson*, 12 B.R. 483 (W.D. Mo. 1981)

Insurance Assessment or insurance premium proceeds

Disability or illness benefits

Fraternal benefit society benefits to $5000, bought over 6 months before filing

Life insurance dividends, loan value or interest to $5000, bought over 6 months before filing

Life insurance proceeds if policy owned by woman & insures her husband

Life insurance proceeds if policy owned by unmarried woman and insures her father or brother

Stipulated insurance premiums

Unmatured life insurance policy
377.090
513.430(10)(c)
513.430(8)
513.430(8)
376.530
376.550

377.330
513.430(7)

Miscellaneous Alimony, child support to $500 per month

Property of business partnership
513.430(10(d) 358.250

Pensions – Employees of cities with 100,000 or more people

ERISA-qualified benefits needed for support (only payments being received)
Firefighters
Highway & transportation employees
Police Department employees
State employees
Teachers
71.207
513.430(10)(e)
87.090, 87.365, 87.485
104.250
86.190, 86.353, 86.493, 86.780
104.540
169.090

Personal Property Appliances, household goods, furnishings, clothing, books, crops, animals & musical instruments to $1,000

Burial grounds to 1 acre or $100

Health aids

Jewelry to $500

Motor vehicle to $1000

Personal injury causes of action

Wrongful death recoveries for person debtor depended on
513.430(1)
214.190
513.430(9)
513.430(2)
513.430(5)
***In re Mitchell*, 73 B.R. 93**
(E.D. Mo. 1987)
513.430(11)

Public benefits AFDC

Social security

Unemployment compensation

Veterans' benefits

Workers' compensation
513.430(10(a)
513.430(10)(a)
288.380(10(l), 53.430(10)(c)
513.430(10)(b)
287.260

Tools of Trade Implements, books & tools of trade to $2000 513.430(4)

Wages Minimum 75% of earned but unpaid wages (90% for head of family); bankruptcy judge may authorize more for low-income debtors

Wages of servant or common laborer to $90

525.030
513.470

WILD CARD $1250 of any property if head of family, else $400; head of family may claim an additional $250 per child 513.430(3), 513.440

Florida exemptions

FLORIDA STATE EXEMPTION STATUTES FEDERAL BANKRUPTCY EXEMPTIONS ARE NOT AVAILABLE.

All law references are to Florida Statutes Annotated unless otherwise noted.

ASSET EXEMPTION LAW PROVISION

Homestead Real or personal property including mobile or modular home to unlimited value; property cannot exceed ½ acre in municipality or 160 contiguous acres elsewhere; spouse or child or deceased owner may claim homestead exemption --- May file homestead declaration

Property held as tenancy by the entirety may be exempt against debts owed by only one spouse
222.01, 222.02,
222.03, 222.05,
Constitution 10-4
222.01
In re Avins, 19 B.R. 736 (S.D. Fla. 1982)

Insurance Annuity contract proceeds; does not include lottery winnings

Death benefits payable to a specific beneficiary, not the deceased's estate

Disability or illness benefits

Fraternal benefit society benefits, if received before 10/1/96

Life insurance cash surrender value
222.14; *In re Pizzi*, 153 B.R.
357 (S.D. Fla. 1982)
222.13
222.18
632.619
222.14

Miscellaneous Alimony, child support needed for support

Damages to employees for injuries in hazardous occupations

Pre-need funeral contract deposits

Property of business partnership
222.201
769.05
497.413(8)
620.68

Pensions
see also WAGES
County officers, employees
ERISA-qualified benefits
Firefighters
Highway patrol officers
Police officers
State officers, employees
Teachers
122.15
222.21(2)
175.241
321.22
185.25
121.131
238.15

Personal property; Any personal property to $1,000 (Husband & wife may double)

Health aids

Motor vehicle to $1000 Constitution 10-4; *In re Hawkins*, 51 B.R. 348
(S.D. Fla. 1985)
222.25
222.25

Public benefits Crime victims' compensation unless seeking to discharge debt for treat of injury incurred during the crime

Hazardous occupation injury recoveries

Public assistance

Social security

Unemployment compensation

Veterans' benefits

Workers' compensation
960.14
769.05
222.201
222.201
222.201, 443.051(2), (3)
222.201, 744.626

440.22

Tools of trade NONE

Wages $100 of wages for heads of family up to $500 per week either unpaid or paid and deposited into bank account for up to 6 months

Federal government employees pension payments needed for support and received 3 months prior
222.11
222.21

WILD CARD --- SEE PERSONAL PROPERTY

Arkansas exemptions

ARKANSAS STATE EXEMPTION STATUTES FEDERAL BANKRUPTCY EXEMPTIONS ARE AVAILABLE

All law references are to Arkansas Code Annotated unless otherwise noted.

ASSET EXEMPTION LAW PROVISION

HOMESTEAD

Choose option 1 or 2, NOT BOTH

1.) For head of family: real or personal property used as residence, to an unlimited value; property cannot exceed ¼ acre in city, town, village or **80** acres elsewhere. If property is between ¼ - **1** acre in city, town or village, or **80** - **160** acres elsewhere, to **$2,500**; no homestead may exceed **1** acre in city, town or village, or **160** acres elsewhere (husband and wife may not double, *In re Stevens*, **829 F.2d 693 (8th Cir. 1987)**) **Constitution 9-3, 9-4, 9-5; 16-66-210, 16-66-218(b)(3), (4)**

2.) Real or personal property used as residence, to **$800** if single; **$1,250** if married **16-66-218(a)(1)**

INSURANCE Annuity contract **23-79-134**

Disability benefits **23-79-133**

Fraternal benefit society benefits **23-74-403**

Group life insurance **23-79-132**

Life, health, accident or disability cash value or proceed paid or due
(limited to the **$500** exemption provided by §§ **9-1** and **9-2** of the Arkansas Constitution, *In re Holt*, **97 B.R. 997 (W.D. Ark. 1988).**) **16-66-209**

Life insurance proceeds if clause prohibits proceeds from being used to pay beneficiary's creditors **23-79-131**

Life insurance proceeds or avails if beneficiary isn't the insured **23-79-131**

Mutual assessment life or disability benefits to **$1,000 23-79-114**
Stipulated insurance premiums **23-71-112**

MISCELLANEOUS Property of business partnership **4-42-502**

PENSIONS Disabled firefighters **24-11-814**
Disabled police officers **24-11-417**
Firefighters **24-10-616**
IRA deposits to $20,000b if deposited over **1** year before filing bankruptcy **16-66-218(b)(16)**
Police officers **24-10-616**
School employees **24-7-715**
State police officers **24-6-202, 24-6-205, 24-6-223**

PERSONAL PROPERTY Burial plot to **5** acres, in lieu of homestead option **2 16-66-207, 16-66-218(a)(1)**

Clothing **Constitution 9-1, 9-2**
Motor vehicle to **$1,200 16-66-218(a)(2)**

Wedding bands; any diamond can't exceed ½ carat **16-66-218(a)(3)**

PUBLIC BENEFITS Aid to blind, aged, disabled, AFDC **20-76-430**

Crime victim's compensation unless seeking to discharge debt for treatment of injury incurred during the crime **16-90-716(e)**

Unemployment compensation **11-10-109**

Workers' compensation **11-9-110**

TOOLS OF TRADE Implements, books and tools of trade to **$750 16-66-218(a)(4)**

WAGES Earned but unpaid wages due for **60** days; in no event under **$25** per week **6-66-208, 16-66-218(b)(6)**

WILD CARD $500 of any personal property if married or head of family; else **$200 Constitution 9-1, 9-2; 16-66-218(b)(1), (2)**

Note that Arkansas is one of the states that allows debtor to claim federal exemptions.

If any federal or state exemption is unclear to debtor, go to internet or public library and read the statute listed next to the exemption including footnotes and comments. The statute notations are also important because the required forms ask for statutory authority for the exemption.

The wide variation in state allowed exemptions is difficult to overcome other than by simply waiting to file a Chapter 7 Bankruptcy until the residency requirement is fulfilled if practical (a period over which debtor call stall creditors). The state exemptions allowed are very important in helping the debtor to decide whether to file Chapter 7 Bankruptcy or continue struggling with an oppressive load of debt.

Once the tough decision to proceed with a Chapter 7 Bankruptcy has been made, the balance of the filing process involves filling out the required forms and attending the court hearings scheduled by the relevant bankruptcy court. The initial filing of the bankruptcy petition with the court clerk bars creditors from further collection activities. The court clerk will notify debtor of each scheduled hearing date and time. The court will appoint a bankruptcy trustee to handle final distribution of none-exempt debtor assets to creditors and will conduct a meeting with creditors which debtor is required to attend and answer relevant questions from creditors and/or the appointed trustee. At the creditors' meeting any challenge to debt discharge by any creditor must be voiced and filed with the appointed trustee and the court at which time debtor will be officially notified of the challenge. If the challenge is not frivolous, the debtor may resort to hiring a bankruptcy lawyer. Most challenges result from dishonest declarations from debtor when filling out the required forms. If there are no challenges, and usually there are none, the discharge is virtually automatic pursuant to a few simple questions asked by the judge and directed to the debtor. The creditors involved at the creditors' meeting will be those creditors listed by the debtor when filling out the required forms and/or any other creditor with a legal interest. Creditors generally do not attend the court scheduled meetings and hearing unless raising a challenge to debt discharge. If there are no challenges, the debtor's debts will be discharged in bankruptcy and the court will notify both debtor and creditors. The debtor's debt discharge in bankruptcy is a public record and will be reported to credit reporting agencies.

The overwhelming majority of Chapter 7 bankruptcies involve debtors who have no significant assets that are not exempt. Thus, taking Chapter 7 bankruptcy usually involves taking two required courses conducted by approved providers and filing the required certificates of completion; obtaining and filling out all required Chapter 7 forms; filing the filled out forms and paying a total of $299.00 filing fees (debtor may seek permission from court to pay the fees in four installments or for waiver of fees if financially destitute); attending court scheduled meetings with creditors and the court appointed trustee; and attending the court scheduled hearing wherein the judge decides whether or not to grant discharge of debts (virtually automatic if debtor qualifies to file a Chapter 7 bankruptcy and debtor has not attempted to deceive creditors or the court).

Some of the required Chapter 7 Bankruptcy forms and questions may not apply to a particular debtor and the non-relevant forms or questions will be readily apparent. At first glance, the required forms appear daunting but actually are not difficult to fill out accurately if a little preparation and organization is done beforehand.

Step one:

Gather up all documents having to do with every debt owed and sort into two stacks ---- one for secured creditors such as mortgage holders and auto loans; and one for unsecured creditors such as credit cards and miscellaneous unpaid bills where no collateral is involved.

Step two:

Add up the total debt for each of the two stacks to determine total liabilities in each stack and a single total for both stacks. Check to make sure the document representing each creditor in each stack shows the name of the creditor, creditor's address and phone number, the date debt was established and the dollar value of the debt, the balance due on the debt and the periodic payment amount. If any of this information is missing, call the creditor and write down the information on the creditor's document and place back in the stack the document was pulled from. If a creditor is a collection agency who purchased the debt from the original or subsequent creditor, make sure the collection agency document lists the original creditor. If not, call the collection agency and get the information. They are required by law to provide the name of the original creditor. If the collection agency begins a collection effort, tell the agency you have filed bankruptcy and not to contact you again. You do not have to listen to any threats or insults.

Step three:

Schedule and complete the two required instructional courses and obtain proof of completion. The information compiled during steps one and two will be reviewed during the instructional courses. Compile a list of personal assets (real estate, personal property, monies owed to you, cash on hand, bank deposits, stocks, bonds, checking accounts, retirement benefits, insurance policies, wages earned but not yet paid, and everything else that has any value and review carefully. Determine the fair market value of each item listed and post the value next to the item. Do not overprice items like clothing, books, furniture, appliances, jewelry, and other items where the fair market value is subjective guesswork. Use blue book values for automobiles, trucks, etc. Check classified ads for items like boats, motors, trailers, computers, printers, electronic equipment, entertainment assets, and other items where realistic and easily verifiable fair market value can be established. For odd and miscellaneous items, use garage sale values.

Step four:

Go to a legal stationery store or download from the internet at www.uscourts.gov/bkforms/index.html to obtain a complete set of required forms for a Chapter 7 Bankruptcy proceeding. Make copies to use in case one or more forms must be redone. Relax at home and carefully review each form and consider each question that applies to you and determine whether you have the answer at your fingertips. If not, you must figure out a way to get the information to answer the question, then write down the information on a notepad which you keep with your other organized paperwork. Be honest with yourself during the entire preparation process. You do not want a creditor challenge.

Step five:

Review again the federal and state allowed exemptions and make an orderly list making sure you have arrived at a fair market value for each item. The market value is important because of maximum dollar value allowed for certain classes of exemptions. Then choose either federal or state allowed exemptions or state exemptions plus limited federal exemption not covered by state exemptions. Choose based upon which set of exemptions allows you to retain the largest portion of your assets. Then, review the lists several times and make sure everything is accounted for and is correctly described with a fair market value.

Step six:

Fill out the required forms making absolutely sure you list the required information for every debt and fully describe every exempt asset in the proper space on the forms. Any exempt asset not listed will not be exempted. Do not forget to list every unpaid bill as a debt. Then review your receipt files, checkbook ledger, and canceled checks, etc. to make sure you have remembered every outstanding debt and to verify your values assigned to various assets. Make a personal copy of all forms filled out.

Step seven:

Sign and date the required set of forms where indicated. Take the completed forms to the local federal bankruptcy court and file with the clerk's office. Either pay the required fees or apply for installment payments. If financially destitute (unable to pay the fees due to level of poverty) apply for waiver of fees. Then, simply wait to be contacted by the court clerk regarding court scheduled creditor meetings and final hearing date.

Note that debtor must furnish the above information whether or not represented by an attorney. If represented, in most cases, a paralegal will ask the debtor the form questions and simply write in the debtor's answers.

Check with the clerk's office at the local federal bankruptcy court to make sure that you have a complete set of the required Chapter 7 Bankruptcy forms including any new form for filing of proof of completion of the two required debtor instructional courses described above. Some local federal bankruptcy courts are now supplying the complete set of required Chapter 7 forms because a large number of debtors are filing a Chapter 7 bankruptcy without hiring an attorney. The required forms other than certificates of required courses completion are:

VOLUNTARY PETITION FORM

This is the master form declaring debtor's intention to file a Chapter 7 Bankruptcy. Husband and wife may file a joint petition and pay the same fees as an individual debtor. The form requires personal information for debtor (or debtors if husband and wife filing jointly), certification of certain entries, prior bankruptcy within 8 years case information, and debtor(s) signatures plus attorney information and signature. Fill out the form as follows:

Under UNITED STATES BANKRUPTCY COURT heading, enter the judicial district where the court is located if not pre-printed on form. If district is not known to debtor, call the court clerk for district identification.

In the spaces provided, enter the name and address information for each debtor if joint petition and last four numbers of each debtor's social security number. Enter all other names used by each debtor during the past eight years in space provided. If no other names used, enter NONE. Then, enter county of residence for each debtor and mailing address if different from street address.

For all spaces pertaining to a business, leave blank. If a business is involved in the Chapter 7 petition, representation by an attorney is highly recommended. This information packet is not intended for a business.

Under the heading CHAPTER OF BANKRUPTCY CODE UNDER WHICH THE

PETITION IS FILED, check "Chapter 7." Under NATURE OF DEBTS, check "Debts are primarily consumer debts."

Under FILING FEE, check the box indicating how debtor(s) wish to pay the filing fee. Ignore entries for Chapter 11 Debtors.

Under heading STASTICAL/ADMINISTRATIVE INFORMATION, check the top box if you believe there will be any assets to distribute to unsecured creditors after you claim your allowed exemptions and after debts involving collateral such as auto loans and mortgages are subtracted from your total assets. If you do not think so, check the bottom box.

Under the heading ESTIMATED NUMBER OF CREDITORS, check either box 1-49 or 50-99. It would be extremely rare for any husband and wife to owe more than 99 different creditors. Generally, the total number of creditors will be less than 49. The other boxes are for businesses. Under the heading ESTIMATED ASSETS, enter the total value of all your assets calculated in Step three. Under the heading ESTIMATED LIABILITIES, enter your total debt calculated in Steps one and two.

On page 2 under the heading VOLUNTARY PETITION, enter name(s) of debtor(s). If either husband or wife or business partner has filed a bankruptcy petition during the past eight years, enter the required information in the spaces provided. If not, enter NONE.

Under the heading, EXHIBIT A, leave blank. Under the heading, EXHIBIT B, debtor(s) sign and date. If joint petition, both husband and wife sign and date signature. Under the heading, EXHIBIT C, check the "no" box. This question is for a business. Under the heading EXHIBIT D, check the top box if individual debtor, check the bottom box if husband and wife filing jointly. There is a required two-page form for Exhibit D. If husband and wife filing jointly, both must fill out a separate Exhibit D form which pertains to credit counseling within six months prior to filing a Chapter 7 bankruptcy. Very carefully, read and consider the specific wording in each of the five boxes. Check the box that applies to individual debtor, sign and date. Remember, if filing jointly, husband and wife must each complete a separate Exhibit D form.

Under the heading INFORMATION REGARDING THE DEBTOR – VENUE, check only the top box. Under the heading CERTIFICATION BY A DEBTOR WHO RESIDES AS A TENANT OF RESIDENTIAL PROPERTY, check each box that applies and enter the required information. The four boxes pertain to debtors who rent from a landlord who has a judgment permitting eviction at the time of filing of a Chapter 7 Bankruptcy. The debtor may avoid eviction by checking all four boxes and making the required money deposit with the court and serving notice on the landlord. The logic is that after debt discharge, debtor will be able to make timely rent payments including past due payments.

     Page 3 of this form is only a signature page. Under the heading SIGNATURE(S) OF DEBTOR(S) (INDIVIDUAL/JOINT), debtor signs and dates and enters telephone number. If joint petition, both husband and wife must sign. Leave the rest of this page blank.

SCHEDULE A --- REAL PROPERTY FORM

     Before attempting to fill out Schedule A, read the instructions for schedules A through J to avoid entering required information on the wrong schedule. Schedule A is intended to tally all real estate interests that can be considered a debtor asset other than executory contracts, unexpired leases and timeshare interests (which are entered on Schedule G).

Under the column heading DESCRIPTION AND LOCATION OF PROPERTY, enter NONE if debtor(s) possess no real estate interests or other real property interests. Otherwise, enter the description and location of the real estate interest wherein debtor(s) have the most equity. Under the heading NATURE OF DEBTOR'S INTEREST IN PROPERTY, enter owner if debtor(s) purchased property; or co-tenant owner if owned jointly with someone other than spouse; or life estate if debtor(s) have a legal right to live in property until death; or future interest and describe exact nature of such interest; or "equitable rights exercisable for debtor(s) benefit" and describe such equitable rights.

Under the column heading HUSBAND, WIFE, JOINT OR COMMUNITY, if debtor is married or if husband and wife are filing joint petition, enter H if property titled to husband, W if titled to W, J if titled jointly, or C if married and living in a "marital community property state."

Under column heading CURRENT VALUE OF DEBTOR'S INTEREST IN PROPERTY, WITHOUT DEDUCTING ANY SECURED CLAIM OR EXEMPTION, enter the fair market value of the debtor's interest in the property without regard for mortgages or liens and whether any portion of debtor(s) interest will be claimed as exempt property under either state or federal exemptions.

Under the column heading AMOUNT OF SECURED CLAIM, enter the dollar amount of any mortgage or lien.

Then, repeat the above described entries for any other real property interests and add up the total and post in the space provided on form. Most Chapter 7 debtors will have only one or two real property interests.

SCHEDULE B PERSONAL PROPERTY

This schedule is essentially filled out exactly like Schedule A and covers personal property rather than real estate or other real property. The schedule lists each category of personal property which simplifies the filling out process. In addition, the current value of personal property will be previously calculated in Step three. Schedule B is a three-page form with 35 line items describing various categories of personal property. For each of the thirty-five line items, enter NONE if debtor(s) own no such personal property. Under the DESCRIPTION AND LOCATION OF PROPERTY column, enter where property is located, state if another person is holding the property for debtor(s) including that person's name and address, state if property is being held for a minor child including only the child's initials and the name and address of child's parent or guardian. Do not disclose the child's name. Read and follow directions on the form concerning any necessary continuation sheets. In the column indicating how property is titled or owned and the column indicating value of debtor(s) interest, fill out the same way as Schedule A. In calculating value of debtor(s) interest, do not deduct secured claims nor exemptions.

SCHEDULE C PROPERTY CLAIMED AS EXEMPT

Schedule C is nothing more than a listing of property claimed by debtor in accordance with state law where debtor satisfies the residency requirement to be eligible to claim state exemptions. To complete Schedule C, first obtain a list of property exemptions for your state of residency. If your state allows some federal exemptions not allowed under state exemptions, obtain a list of federal exemptions and compare both lists to determine what exemptions you are eligible to claim. Remember that some states do not allow any federal exemptions if state exemptions are claimed. Review the sample exemption lists above for Missouri, Florida and Arkansas. Note that the state statute which allows each exemption is usually printed next to the exemption.

Also remember that a complete list of all debtor(s)' assets was compiled during Step three above along with the fair market value of each asset. Note the four column headings for Schedule C: Description of Property; Specify Law Providing Each Exemption; Value of Claimed Exemption; and Current Value of Property Without Deducting Exemption.

At the top of Schedule C, enter name(s) of

Debtor(s) and case number if known. Then, if you are claiming a homestead exemption, check the boxes that apply to the homestead exemption claimed. (remember, to obtain a list of state and federal exemptions, go to the internet or public library and use the search phrase: "state property exemptions allowed during Chapter 7 bankruptcy proceeding," and then "federal property exemptions allowed during Chapter 7 bankruptcy proceeding").

Now, all the information is fully organized to fill out the balance of Schedule C. For each exempt item, enter exempt property description in the first column, the state statute allowing exemption in the second column, the value of exemption claimed (how much of total value is allowed as an exemption) in the third column, and, in the fourth column, list the current value of each property item listed WITHOUT deducting the exemption amount.

By now, it should be apparent that the name(s) of debtor(s) and the case number if known must be entered on every schedule form and any continuation sheets. Thus, this instruction need not be repeated.

SCHEDULE D CREDITORS HOLDING SECURED CLAIMS

A secured claim is just another way of describing a debt where the creditor has a collateral right to repossess the property involved if debtor defaults on the contractual payment schedule. In legalese, this is referred to as a secured claim or security interest. In a Chapter 7 bankruptcy proceeding, all creditors holding secured claims may repossess the property involved whether real estate or personal property such that the appointed trustee cannot sell the property and distribute the proceeds to other creditors. Such secured claims generally involve real estate mortgages and motor vehicle loans. Occasionally, secured claims can also involve furniture loans, jewelry, boats, motors, tools, and other expensive items purchased on credit with creditor repossession rights if debtor defaults on payment schedule or fails to maintain contractually required insurance on the property.

In Steps one and two above, a complete list of all debts was compiled along with creditor addresses, account numbers, telephone numbers, date each debt was established, payment schedule, balance of debt not repaid, the current market value of the property for which the debt was established, and the periodic payment schedule. Steps one and two makes filling out the balance of all required schedules quick and simple.

If debtor(s) do not have any secured creditors, simply check the box above the row of nine columns. Otherwise, fill out Schedule D as follows:

In the first column, enter each secured creditor alphabetically including for each creditor an account number, and mailing address with zip code. If a creditor is a minor child, read paragraph 2 of form instructions and make entries accordingly.

For EACH creditor entered, in the spaces and boxes provided across from each creditor, check indicated box if there is someone else liable for debt other than spouse; enter a capital letter to indicate who is responsible for debt (H for husband, W for wife, J for both husband and wife, or C if living in a community property state and spouse in not joining in the Chapter 7 bankruptcy proceeding). Then, for each creditor, in the column provided, enter the date the debt was incurred, the type of claim (mortgage, lien, etc.), describe the property subject to repossession (all or some divisible portion), and the fair market value of property subject to repossession.

Next, check the appropriate box to indicate if the debt is contingent (the debt will be initially incurred depending upon some future event), unliquidated (a definite amount still owed by debtor) or disputed (debtor and creditor disagree about the debt itself or the exact amount of unpaid balance).

Next, in the column indicated, enter the unpaid debt amount without regard to any collateral considerations.

Finally, in the last column, enter the unsecured portion of debt. For example, the unpaid balance of a car loan is $3,500 but the fair market value of the car is only $1,500. The unsecured portion of the car loan debt is $2,000.

Now, calculate a total for each of the last two columns on form. **If the continuation sheet is necessary to list all secured creditors, only use the SUBTOTAL box provided and use the TOTAL box provided at the bottom of the**

continuation form.

SCHEDULE E CREDITORS HOLDING UNSECURED PRIORITY CLAIMS

Creditors holding unsecured **priority** claims are next in line to be paid by the court appointed trustee from any monies remaining in the debtor(s)' bankruptcy estate after creditors holding secured claims have been paid. Schedule E is a three-page form listing the various categories of such priority claims. Review each category and if no category of unsecured priority claims applies to debtor(s), check the appropriate box on first page just above the category listing. Ignore the categories that apply to a business.

Under TYPES OF PRIORITY CLAIMS, check the box for DOMESTIC SUPPORT OBLIGATIONS if any type of alimony or child support is applicable to debtor. Check the box for DEPOSITS BY INDIVIDUALS if debtor(s) are holding any type of prepayment or security deposit involving real estate sale, lease or rental or for services which were not rendered. Check the box for TAXES AND CERTAIN OTHER DEBTS OWED TO GOVERNMENTAL UNITS including penalties if applicable to debtor(s). Check the box for CLAIMS FOR DEATH OR PERSONAL INJURY WHILE DEBTOR WAS INTOXICATED if this category applies to debtor(s). The remaining categories apply to a business.

    On page three of form, in the appropriate columns, enter name of person or entity to whom debt is owed, account number if any, and the correct address including zip code; check if there is a co-debtor; enter the H or W, or J, or C indicating who is liable for debt (read prior instruction); check whether the debt is contingent, unliquidated or disputed; the dollar value of claim; the amount of claim entitled to priority; and amount, if any, not entitled to priority. In the space provided, indicate the number of continuation sheets, if any. Finally, total the last three columns according to printed instructions at bottom of page three (use the TOTAL boxes only on last page if continuation sheets are necessary).

SCHEDULE F CREDITORS HOLDING UNSECURED NONPRIORITY CLAIMS

Schedule F merely continues the listing of creditors and pertains only to unsecured priority debts such as credit cards, personal loans where no collateral is involved, unpaid utility bills, etc.

Schedule F is filled out just like Schedule E with respect to the eight columns on the schedule with one additional bit of information: whether the creditor has a legal right of set-off. If debtor(s) do not know whether set-off applies to creditor, do not make a setoff entry. Set-off is defined as follows:

Right To Set-off By A Creditor

In a bankruptcy action, a creditor with a state law right of set-off, may be entitled to offset a mutual debt owing by the creditor to the debtor, that arose before the commencement of the case, against a claim of the creditor against the debtor that arose before the commencement of the claim, except to the extent that:

> **"(1) the claim of the creditor against the debtor is disallowed;**
>
> **(2) the claim was transferred, by an entity other than the debtor, to the creditor after the commencement date of the bankruptcy filing; or within 90 days before the filing of the bankruptcy while the debtor was insolvent; or the debt owed by the debtor to the creditor was incurred within 90 days before the filing of the**

bankruptcy and for the sole purpose of obtaining a right of set-off against the debtor."

In less complex language this says that if a creditor has a claim for $1,000 against a debtor, but at the same time owes the debtor $500, the creditor can write off the $500 owing to the debtor against the $1000 the debtor owes the creditor if both debts were incurred at least 90 days prior to the debtor filing bankruptcy and no intent to defraud other creditors was involved in the creation of either debt.

SCHEDULE G EXECUTORY CONTRACTS AND UNEXPIRED LEASES

An executory contract is a contract where the contract is in progress but not completed at the time debtor files bankruptcy such as unexpired leases, timeshares, or any other contract where financial consideration is involved for something started but ongoing until a certain date and the debtor has a future vested interest that has monetary value. For example: an unexpired lease requires the lessor to allow lessee to occupy the property until the lease expires for a fixed lump sum or periodic payment without regard to the present or future lease value of the property. Another example: debtor sells on a commission basis a hundred thousand dollars of goods or services to be delivered or performed partially at time of sale and partially in the future and debtor's commission of 5% is to be paid as the sales contract is being fulfilled. The buyer pays one half down and the balance is due when contract is fulfilled. The debtor files bankruptcy and is entitled to a commission of $5,000 three months later. Another example: Debtor owns a time share for a ten year period for annual payment of $1,000. The value of the time share escalates to $2,000 per year after one year but debtor is only obligated to pay $1,000 for another nine years. Debtor's interest in the time share is 100% greater during the second year of the timeshare contract. There are many other examples of executory contracts.

  And, of course, the debtor can be the lessor of various types of property and have a future monetary interest; or might have partially fulfilled a service contract where monies will be paid debtor at future date. This is what Schedule

G captures for the trustee's evaluation of the debtor's bankruptcy estate subject to distribution to creditors.

Keeping the definition of an executory contract in mind, fill out Schedule G as instructed on the form listing each executory contract including all parties to the contract, mailing addresses with zip codes, specific contract description, nature of debtor's interest including nonresidential property lease(s), account numbers that apply, and contract number for any government executory contract.

Most debtors filing Chapter 7 bankruptcy will not be involved in executory contracts and should simply check the box below the form instructions.

SCHEDULE H CO-DEBTORS

Schedule H requires the names and addresses of any co-debtor such as co-signers or guarantors of any debt listed on any schedule. In addition, if the debtor lived in a community property state during the eight years prior to filing Chapter 7, Schedule H requires the name of debtor's spouse if not a joint Chapter 7 filing, and the name of any former spouse including all other names used by such former spouse while residing with debtor in a community property state during the eight years prior to debtor filing the bankruptcy petition. The community property states are listed on Schedule H with adequate instructions for filling out the form.

SCHEDULES I AND J – CURRENT INCOME AND EXPENSES.

Schedule I captures monthly income and Schedule J captures monthly expenses. Income and expense calculations must all be converted to a monthly average regardless of when income is actually received or when expenses are paid. The forms are self-explanatory and need no interpretation or rewording. Read the printed instructions on each schedule carefully before starting to fill out the forms. Spouse income must be included for every married debtor filing Chapter 7 Bankruptcy.

The forms are poorly designed and must be read slowly and carefully before filling out to avoid wasting time and having to replace forms due to entry errors. Note that at the top of

Schedule I there is very little space on the form to enter the relationship of all dependents and their ages such that a continuation sheet may be necessary to provide this information. Be sure that any such continuation sheet is identified with names(s) of debtors and case number if known.

SUMMARY OF SCHEDULES FORM

This form is basically a summary sheet to check that Schedules A, B, C, D, E, F, G, H, I, and J have been filled out and attached to the master petition form, and that the number of continuation forms for each schedule is noted for the convenience of the court and trustee when reviewing the Chapter 7 filing. This form also recaps the total dollars calculated as the schedules were completed. Therefore, it is merely a check to make sure all necessary schedules are attached and total dollars have been recapped in one place.

STATISTICAL SUMMARY OF CERTAIN LIABILITIES AND RELATED DATA

This form is another summary form that requires only copying information from the previous schedule forms for statistical analysis and tabulation for governmental purposes in tracking bankruptcy data. Since this form requires only posting of total dollar figures from schedules filled out as part of filing Chapter 7 bankruptcy, no additional instructions beyond those printed on the form are needed or useful.

DECLARATION CONCERNING DEBTOR'S SCHEDULES

This final form is a declaration under oath that the information debtor entered into Schedules A through J was accurate to the best of debtor(s)' knowledge and belief and includes debtor(s)' final tally of the total pages within the petition master form and all attached schedules and summaries. Simply enter total sheets, debtor(s)' name(s) and case number if known, signature(s) of debtor(s) and date signed in the spaces printed on form. Disregard the other two declarations as they do not apply to debtor(s) filing their own non-business Chapter 7 bankruptcy.

A FINAL WORD

The court appointed trustee and debtor(s) can trade exempt property items for non-exempt property if the fair market values are reasonably comparable. The trustee will be anxious to trade hard to sell items for items deemed easier to sell. Also, some secure debts can be reaffirmed such as mortgages and motor vehicle loans, especially if the fair market value is lower than the value of the reaffirmed loan(s). If debtor(s) wish to do some trading of property with the trustee, or to reaffirm one or more debts, the trustee should be informed as soon as possible.

Chapter Two

Filing An Uncontested Divorce

General Information

Family law matters such as divorce, child support, child custody, alimony, etc. are heard and decided in "family law courts" located in most counties within every state. The court name my vary from state to state (Associate Circuit Court; Family Law Court; Domestic Relations Court; etc.). In some states, divorce proceedings are filed in the County Circuit Court.

    To find out where to file for an uncontested divorce, call the County Circuit Clerk's office and ask for the name of the divorce court and where the court is located. Once the designated court is determined, call the court clerk's office (look in telephone directory) and ask if the state requires residence in the state for any period of time before filing for divorce and whether the court requires any pre-approved official court forms in connection with an uncontested divorce. For example, in Missouri, at least one of the parties must have been a resident of Missouri for a full 90 days before filing for a dissolution of marriage; divorce proceedings are heard in the County Circuit Court; and Missouri does require some official court forms to be completed and filed. There is a 30-day waiting period after the court proceedings have begun before a dissolution of marriage can be granted.

Again, uncontested divorce proceedings will vary somewhat from state to state, but the variations are mainly procedural and the forms are not difficult to obtain and file. The filing fee may vary from county to county

A divorce (legally referred to as "dissolution of marriage") is considered an adversarial legal proceeding and as such can be hotly contested. For a contested divorce, both parties should hire an attorney.

On the other hand, if both parties

to the pending divorce agree on the grounds for divorce; and agree concerning the allocation of marital debt between the parties; and agree concerning child custody and child support (if minor children are involved); and agree on spousal support (alimony); and further agree on the division of real and personal property between the parties, the uncontested divorce is merely a legal formality and money spent on attorneys' fees is wasted. It is not uncommon for fees for each party's attorney to exceed $1,500 for handling an uncontested divorce. Thus, if both parties can agree on the terms of the dissolution of marriage, the hard cash savings can be substantial.

The legal paperwork involved may require a combination of court approved pre-printed forms and forms created by the parties. The normal uncontested divorce forms (packet of forms) that must be filed with the court clerk along with the required filing fee includes:

PETITION FOR DISSOLUTION OF MARRIAGE.

The spouse who files the action with the court is called the Petitioner and the responding spouse is called the Respondent. If the parties file jointly to end the marriage, they are called Co-Petitioners.

Some states allow "no fault" divorce, while other states require legal grounds for divorce such as adultery, abandonment, separations due to spousal misconduct over an extended period (generally one year prior to divorce action), unreasonable spousal conduct the other spouse cannot be expected to tolerate, living separate and apart for a specified period of time, and general grounds usually described as "irreconcilable differences such that the marriage is irretrievably broken;" and "there is no reasonable likelihood that the marriage can be preserved." In some states (such as Missouri), the grounds for divorce must be substantiated by evidence or witness testimony.

    The petition should state the grounds for divorce in the language approved by the court where the action is filed; the date of the marriage and where the ceremony was conducted; the date the spouses separated; where each spouse lives and works; whether minor children are involved and where they reside; and the proposed custody arrangements. However, it is best to check with the court clerk where the action is filed to establish exactly what the Petition must contain and the court approved wording; what court approved forms are provided; and the schedule of forms that must be attached to the Petition which generally include:

A STATEMENT OF INCOME AND EXPENSES

This schedule documents income and expenses for each spouse including each source of income and description of all expenses by category. Every source of income whether taxable or tax free must be listed for each spouse in separate columns. The same is true for expenses.

A STATEMENT OF MARITAL PROPERTY AND MARITAL DEBT AND PROPOSED SEPARATION AGREEMENT

This schedule must fully describe the marital property (property acquired during the marriage as opposed to property owned by spouses prior to the marriage) whether real or personal property, and the marital debt associated with such property; how the property will be equitably allocated between the parties; and how marital debt will be equitably allocated between the parties.

A PARENTING PLAN (when minor children are involved)

This schedule sets forth the

agreement between the parties as to custody rights and visitation rights by the non-custodial spouse for each minor child; child support allocation between the parties; and visitation rights for grandparents.

STATE DEPARTMENT OF HEALTH CERTIFICATE OF DISSOLUTION OF MARRIAGE

This schedule records the divorce for record keeping purposes for the benefit of the parties and for all legal and governmental needs.

FAMILY COURT FILING CERTIFICATE

This schedule lists any other pending action(s) between the parties involved in the dissolution of marriage so that potential conflicts of interest may be avoided.

JUDGMENT OF DISSOLUTION

This schedule is prepared for the judge to sign to end the marriage. Ask court clerk for format and proper wording; or ask the clerk to let you review an uncontested divorce case file to ascertain the proper format and official wording. Some courts may furnish a blank schedule for Judgment of Dissolution of Marriage.

The spouse filing the Petition attaches all required schedules to the Petition and delivers the packet to the court clerk along with the filing fee required by the court. If the parties are filing as Co-Petitioners, the case will be docketed in the court and the parties will be notified by the court clerk as to when the case will be called before the judge.

     If the parties are not filing as Co-Petitioners, the responding spouse (called Respondent) must file an answer to the Petition for Dissolution upon being formally served with the petition by the filing spouse (called Petitioner). Service may be completed by Petitioner if Respondent does not object; or by a process server; or by publication (newspaper notice) in accordance with state law. Respondent generally has 20 to 30 days (set by the court) to file an answer. If the answer is not filed by the filing deadline, Petitioner may ask the court for a default judgment and granting of the dissolution as set forth in the Petition. Individuals serving abroad in the military are protected from such default judgments. When sending filings or correspondence to the court, direct the mail to Clerk's Office, name of court and court's address.

The Responding spouse should file a brief answer that clearly states that Respondent adopts and fully agrees with all statements contained in Petitioner's Petition for Dissolution of Marriage and all attachments. Use the format below and Respondent's answer can be captioned "Respondent's Answer to Petition for Dissolution of Marriage."

When filing a court document in a format created by the parties as opposed to a court approved and/or required pre-printed format, use this layout:

In the (name of court) for the (name of county), (name of state)

In Re: the Marriage of:

(name of filing spouse), Petitioner,
v.
(name of responding spouse), Respondent.

Case number_____ (enter if known)

(describe document being filed) (example)
   "Respondent's Answer to Petition

For Dissolution of Marriage"

Comes now Respondent and with respect to the above captioned document states to the court:

(enter the text narrative of document being filed) following the foregoing instructions for Petition, Answer, and attached schedules. It is not necessary to repeat the court heading information on attachments to Petition; but name and exhibit number of each attachment should be listed below the Certificate of Service signature (see example below)

Respectfully submitted,

(signature)

Name
address
telephone number
email (if any)

Certificate of Service

The undersigned hereby certifies that a true and complete copy of the foregoing document was mailed with first class postage prepaid to (name of non-filing spouse) at (address) on the _____ day of _____, 20_____.

_____
(signature of filing spouse)

Date _____

Attachments:

Exhibit A, (name of schedule) _____
Number of pages _____
Exhibit B, (name of schedule) _____
Number of pages _____
Exhibit C, (name of schedule) _____
Number of pages _____
etc.

Note: be sure and post exhibit identification on each attached schedule and assign page numbers for each schedule.

The judge can modify the agreements between the parties if deemed not equitable by the judge including child custody and support, spousal support, division of property, and allocation of marital debt.

Therefore, it is prudent for the parties to an uncontested divorce to keep judicial modification in mind when drafting all agreements to be submitted to the court --- especially child support allocation between the parties and visitation rights. Remember, the court is always supposed to protect the interests of minor children when dissolving marriages.

WHAT TO DO WHEN YOU GO TO COURT HEARING

Both parties will be notified by the court clerk when the uncontested divorce hearing is scheduled to be heard before the judge. Attend the hearing as scheduled and when the bailiff calls your case number, answer "Petitioner and Respondent" (or "Co-

Petitioners") are present, Your Honor. Walk briskly to the judge's bench and both parties identify yourselves. Answer any preliminary questions the judge may ask and then the filing party should say, "If it please the Court, Petitioner calls (name of responding party) to the stand.

    Responding spouse should take the stand to be questioned regarding agreement with all statements contained in the Petition for Dissolution of Marriage and all attached schedules.

    The questioning party should say, "Please state your name, address, and occupation for the record." Wait for response, then ask, "Were you married to (name of questioning party) on (date of marriage) in (name of county), (name of state)? Wait for response. Then ask, "Are you this date and time seeking dissolution of said marriage?" Wait for response. Then ask, "Is there any statement in the Petition for Dissolution of said marriage and the attached schedules that you do not agree with?" Responding party should answer, "No." Then ask, "Are you fully in agreement with all the provisions and allocations contained in all the schedules attached to the Petition for Dissolution of said marriage?" Responding party should answer, "Yes." Then ask, "Do said schedules cover specific agreements between Petitioner and Respondent (or Co-Petitioners) concerning (all of the following that are applicable: child custody, child support for (name each minor child), visitation rights, grandparents' visitation rights, spousal support, allocation between the parties

hereto of all marital real and personal property and all marital debts connected therewith?" Responding party should answer. "Yes." Then ask, "Is said marriage irretrievably broken with no reasonable possibility of reconciliation?"
Responding party should answer, "Yes." Then ask, "Do you fully agree with the grounds for dissolving said marriage that are stated in the Petition for Dissolution of said marriage?" Responding party should answer, "Yes."

Questioning party should then say, "I have nothing further, Your Honor."

Wait for judge to respond and then follow any instructions from the judge. The judge may ask for a verbal reading of spousal agreements by questioning party. The judge may order modification of specific portions of spousal agreements to conform to state law and to reasonable equity as viewed by the judge.

After the statutory waiting period required by some state laws, the judge will issue "The Judgment of Dissolution."

Chapter Three

Composing A Living Will

LIVING WILL

MEDICAL POWER OF ATTORNEY

This information packet contains everything necessary for creating a legally sufficient Living Will and Medical Power of Attorney.

A living will is intended to specify in advance and to legally document an individual's wishes concerning whether he/she wants to be kept alive by life sustaining medical devices during an irreversible state of unconsciousness and/or terminal illness/disease from which recovery is not physically possible as determined by the attending physician(s), and during such state of existence he/she is mentally incapacitated.

In the event of your mental incapacitation occurring in the absence of such a living will and medical power of attorney document, a court hearing will generally be required after which your actual wishes may or may not be carried out because neither the court nor the guardian/power of attorney agent appointed by the court will be completely aware of your undocumented intentions.

Following is a "living will and medical power of attorney

appointment." Clearly indicate your wishes in the space(s) provided using a blue ink pen. Before beginning to fill out the form, make copies in case of unintentional wrong entries. Do not scratch out anything on the form. Then, sign before two witnesses and Notary Public. Make a file copy and give original to your medical power of attorney agent (the person you appoint first).

LIVING WILL AND MEDICAL POWER OF ATTORNEY APPOINTMENT

I,_____
being of legal age and of sound mind and under no pressure or attempted

coercion; having been born on _____ and assigned social security number _____ ; do on this _____ day of _____ 20____ hereby appoint as having my "medical power of attorney" as set forth herein, in this my living will, the following named individuals in the sequential order listed:

First choice

_____

Relationship to me

_____

Second choice

_____

Relationship to me

_____

Third choice

_____

Relationship to me

_____

This is my "living will and medical power of attorney appointment" commencing and valid upon my mental incapacitation resulting from a permanent state of unconsciousness or terminal condition as determined by my attending physician(s) or upon a legal determination issued by a court of competent jurisdiction.

My appointed Medical Attorney-in-Fact (Agent) will not be compensated for his/her efforts as Agent.

If a guardian or trustee needs to be appointed for any reason, I hereby appoint such guardian or trustee in the same sequential order as my appointment herein for my Medical Attorney-in-Fact (Agent).

LIFE SUSTAINING EQUIPMENT AND TREATMENTS

Terminal condition: I do____ do not_____ want such care.

Permanently unconscious: I do___ do not___ want such care.

Tube feeding (food/water): I do___ do not___ want such care.

PAIN MEDICATION AND EUTHANASIA

If in a terminal condition or permanently unconscious, and in pain, I do____ do not____ want any and all pain medications administered. If Euthanasia is legal, I do____ do not____ want to utilize it.

ORGAN DONATION

I do____ do not____ want to donate organs for transplant.

I do____ do not____ want to donate organs for research.

OPTIONAL AGENT POWERS

My medical power of attorney agent is

hereby authorized to:

    consent to or refuse my psychiatric care ---
yes_____ no_____;

    make decisions concerning my funeral ----
yes _____ no____;

    authorize my autopsy ---- yes _____ no _____.

I hereby specifically revoke all other "living wills and medical power of attorney appointments" that I may have executed.

My signature

_____

Date _____

Witness:

_____

Date_____

Witness:

_____

Date_____

Notary Public

County of
_____)

State of
_____)s.s.

Before me, a Notary Public, on

_____, appeared _____ and the two witnesses who have signed before me above, who were all personally identified by me. Then,

_____

signed his foregoing "medical power of attorney appointment" in the sight and hearing of me and said two witnesses who were all present with me. Then,

_____

stated in our presence that he executed the foregoing document in accordance with his free will and deed.

Date: _____

Notary Public

_____ (seal)

My Commission expires

_____

Chapter Four

Composing A Power Of Attorney

GENERAL POWER OF ATTORNEY AND/OR LIMITED POWER OF ATTORNEY

This information packet contains everything necessary for creating a legally sufficient General Power of Attorney and/or a Limited Power of Attorney after the filled out document is signed by the person granting the power of attorney before two witnesses and a Notary Public.

Because of the uncertainties of life and unexpected accidents, it is highly advisable to prepare and safely store a legal power of attorney so that your personal wishes are both known and established prior to your untimely and/or unexpected mental incapacitation. The power of attorney you grant may be immediate for a specific purpose and/or limited time; or become valid only upon your mental incapacitation.

When the properly worded power of attorney document is signed before two witnesses and a Notary Public, it is valid in every state. In the event of your mental incapacitation occurring in the absence of such a power of attorney document, a court hearing will generally be required after which your actual wishes may or may not be carried out because neither the court nor the guardian/executor appointed by the court will be completely aware of your undocumented intentions.

Following is a "power of attorney appointment" which can be filled out as either a "general power of attorney" or a "limited power of attorney." Mark with an "X" the "yes" or "no" blanks with a heavy black magic marker to avoid hidden erasures; and, where appropriate, clearly state your intentions in the space(s) provided using a blue ink pen. Before beginning to fill out the form, make copies in case of unintentional wrong entries. Do not scratch out anything on form. Then, sign before witnesses and Notary

Public. Make a file copy and give original to your power of attorney agent (the person you appoint).

POWER OF ATTORNEY

APPOINTMENT

I,_____

being of legal age and of sound mind and under no pressure or attempted coercion; having been born on _____ and assigned social security number _____ ; do on this _____ day of_____ 20___ hereby appoint as having my "power of attorney" the following named individuals in the sequential order listed:

First choice

_____

Relationship to me

_____

Second choice

_____

Relationship to me

_____

Third choice

_____

Relationship to me

_____

This is a "limited power of attorney

appointment" for the specific purpose(s) of

_____
_____
_____
_____
_____

and this appointment expires on the _____ day of

_____ 20_____.

If this is NOT a limited power of attorney, write "Not Applicable" in the four blanks for "limited power of attorney appointment."

This is a "general power of attorney appointment" commencing and valid upon my mental incapacitation as determined by my attending physician or upon a legal determination issued by a court of competent jurisdiction. If this is NOT a "general power of attorney appointment," enter not applicable in the following blank and enter date:

_____

Date_____ 20____

This "general power of attorney appointment" becomes null and void upon my recovery from any period of mental incapacitation as determined by my attending physician. My Attorney-in-Fact (Agent) shall have the following powers:

Manage all my real estate
yes_____   no_____

Manage my personal property
yes_____   no_____

Manage stock and bond transactions
yes_____   no_____

Manage commodities and options
yes_____   no_____

Manage all other financial transactions
yes_____   no_____

Manage my business operations
yes_____   no_____

Handle any insurance transactions
yes_____   no_____

Handle any beneficiary matters
yes_____ no_____

Handle claims/litigation
yes_____ no_____

Handle personal and family maintenance
yes_____ no_____

Handle government benefits
yes_____ no_____

Handle retirement plan transaction
yes_____ no_____

Handle all tax matters
yes_____ no_____

Make property transfers to qualify me for medical assistance programs yes_____   no_____

Make gifts of real and personal property
yes_____   no_____

Gift himself/herself only if Agent is spouse
yes_____   no_____

My appointed Attorney-in-Fact (Agent) will not be compensated for his/her efforts as Agent.

If a guardian or trustee needs to be appointed for any reason, I hereby appoint such guardian or trustee in the same sequential order as my appointment herein for my Attorney-in-Fact (Agent).

I hereby specifically revoke all other "power of attorney appointments" that I may have executed.

My signature

_____

Date _____

Witness:

_____

Date_____

Witness:

_____

Date_____

               Notary Public

County of
_____)

State of
_____)s.s.

Before me, a Notary Public, on

_____,
appeared

_____and
the two witnesses who have signed above, who were all personally identified by me. Then,

_____

signed his foregoing "power of attorney appointment" in the
sight and hearing of me and said two witnesses who were all present with

me. Then,

_____

stated in our presence that he executed the foregoing document in accordance with his free will and deed.

Date:

_____

Notary Public

_____   (seal)

My Commission expires

_____

Chapter Five

Composing A Last Will And Testament

This Information Packet pertains to preparing a final will:

General Background information

The requirements for a legally sufficient last will and testament varies from state to state and distribution of the assets of a deceased individual is governed by state law called "Probate Law." There are generally only three ways that all of a deceased individual's assets can be distributed:

(1) In accordance with a valid will

(2) Through trust fund(s) administration

(3) Through a Probate Court proceeding

Titled property such as real estate and motor vehicles can be passed to a beneficiary without a will or probate by adding the beneficiary to the title with sole right of survivorship.

The easiest and least expensive way to plan for asset distribution pursuant to death is preparation of a valid will. The most expensive way is through a Probate Court proceeding in the absence of a valid will which involves filing fees plus administrative and trustee costs. Trust funds are easy to set up but involve trustee fees.

In the absence of a valid will, all assets distributed by a Probate Court will pass in accordance with state statutory law and such distribution may be radically different than what the deceased individual actually desired.

Variations from state to state as to what constitutes a valid will pertain mostly to how will preparation is witnessed and whether the will signatures must be before a notary public. The individual preparing his/her will should recite personal identity and place of residence; date of birth and social security number; that he/she is of legal age, mentally competent (of sound mind); possesses contractual capacity; and under no duress or attempts at extortion at the time the will is prepared.

Choose a personal representative (will executor) so your assets will be handled and distributed by someone you trust explicitly and specify funeral and burial instructions.

Specifically state that you are revoking all other wills and codicils you may have previously executed. Authorize your executor to pay from your estate all just debts and funeral expenses plus taxes and estate administration expenses.

Authorize your executor to sell,

lease, pledge or otherwise dispose of any real estate in which you have an interest upon your death in order to make distribution to beneficiaries you designate. List personal property only by category such as cash on hand, money deposits, stocks and bonds, other investments, and miscellaneous assets that you wish to bequeath to specific beneficiaries. Do not refer to specific assets because the actual asset inventory is subject to change prior to death.

In the case of only one beneficiary, the will may simply state "all my worldly goods of any nature whatsoever." A simple will with only spouse and children (or a limited number of relatives or friends selected by an unmarried person) as beneficiaries, and where the estate is not large enough to justify an executor, may designate a percentage of the estate to pass to each beneficiary after specific classes of assets bequeathed to certain beneficiaries have been subtracted.

Even for a vast estate, if more than one beneficiary is named, make distribution to beneficiaries by percentage except when you want a specific asset to go undivided to a particular beneficiary. For example, 50% of all my real estate properties to my wife and 50% to my children equally; and all my hunting gear to my son, Adam. State who gets the gift of a beneficiary who does not survive you. This can be done by naming "residuary beneficiaries" within a residuary clause. The residuary clause takes everything not bequeathed to the first named beneficiaries and everything bequeathed to beneficiaries who do not survive you and gives the items to the residuary beneficiaries. Beneficiaries can be named "Per stirpes" so that the gift passes down the bloodline of the deceased beneficiary.

State whether a named executor must post bond or serve without posting bond. Be clear as to whether your executor should be paid for services and reimbursed for expenses and specify a maximum percentage of the estate value (for example: up to 1.5 % of the total estate value). Name an alternate executor in case your first choice dies or chooses not to serve, or becomes incapacitated.

To make your will valid in every state, sign your initials on each page of your will. Sign your will using your complete name at the very bottom of the last page in the presence of three witnesses and a notary public, all of whom signed in the designated blanks, watched you sign and were all present when you signed, and all of whom are not related to you and who are not beneficiaries or have any interest whatsoever in your will.

Specify a legal guardian for minor children, if any, in the event of your spouse's death.

Place your completed will in a safe and fireproof location and tell only your executor and at least one trusted and disinterested friend where the will is located. It is advisable to give your executor a copy of the will or a second original. Do not write on the finished will. Make any future changes by writing a "codicil" (a separate document which explicitly refers to the original will). Sign the codicil in the same manner as the original will.

Pre-printed will formats are not advisable because the will should contain no blanks that do not apply to the completed will, and every page above the official will signature should be completely filled so that nothing can be added by a forger.

The following sample will should be as instructive as a pre-printed will format and make it a simple task to draft an original personal will without blanks or incomplete pages above the official will signature:

LAST WILL AND TESTAMENT OF JOHN DAVID SMITH

I, John David Smith, being 70 years of age, having been born on September 24, 1939 in Truman, Arkansas and now residing at 2700 Hightower Place, Rocky Mountain, Missouri 65072 and assigned social security number 494-82-0903 do on this twenty-seventh day of August, 2010 declare my last will and testament to wit: I am of sound mind and have contractual capacity and I am not under any pressure, duress or attempts at extortion, and I make this will freely and of my own choice. To my wife, Dorothy Ann Smith, I leave all my real

JDS

estate interests in total to dispose of as she sees fit. To my son, John David Smith, Jr., I leave one fifth of all my property other than real estate. To my daughter, Mary Jo Smith, I leave one fifth of all my property other than real estate. To my daughter, Alice Sue Smith, I leave one fifth of all my property other than real estate. To my daughter, Patricia Ruth Smith, I leave one fifth of all my property other than real estate. To my brother, Robert Albert Smith, I leave one fifth of all my property other than real estate. I appoint my Pastor, Joseph Allan Robbins, as my will executor who has agreed to serve without bond and without compensation. In the event that Joseph Allan Robbins dies or becomes incapacitated, I further appoint my

JDS

lifelong friend, Johnny Lee Owens as my alternate will executor who has also agreed to serve without bond and without compensation. I hereby authorize my will executor to sell, lease, pledge, or otherwise dispose of all my real estate should my wife elect to have the cash value of the real estate rather than the property itself. I further authorize my will executor to pay, from my estate out of cash deposits, miscellaneous administration expenses and reimbursement of any expenses other than administrative. It is my desire that my wife handle my funeral and burial as she sees fit and for my will executor to pay funeral and burial expenses from cash deposits. In the event that my wife does not survive me, I appoint my brother, Robert Albert Smith, and his

JDS

wife, Jodi Rebecca Smith, as guardians for my daughter, Patricia Ruth Smith for as long as she remains a minor; and all my real estate interests shall pass to Patricia Ruth Smith per stirpes instead of my deceased wife. I hereby specifically revoke all other wills and codicils that I may have executed.

John David Smith ----

August 27, 2010

Witness: Joe Allen Clark Date: August 27, 2010

Witness: *Robert Lee Anderson on August* 27, 2010

Witness: James Harry Presley   8/27/2010

Notary Public

County of Morgan)
)s.s.
State of Missouri)

    Before me, a Notary Public, appeared John David Smith and the three witnesses who have signed above, who were all personally identified by me. Then, John David Smith signed his foregoing Last Will and Testament in the sight and hearing of me and said three witnesses who were all present with me. John David Smith stated in our presence that he executed the foregoing document as his free will and act.

Date: _____

Notary Public

_____

(seal)

My Commission expires

_____

Chapter Six

Filing A Small Claim

FILING A CLAIM IN SMALL CLAIMS COURT

General Information:

The Small Claims Court in each county is generally a designated division of the Circuit Court or the Associate Circuit Court for a particular county. Call the Circuit Clerk for the county to ascertain where the court is located and the court address and the small claims filing fee.

Small Claim Courts were established to permit individuals to obtain a court order for financial damages resulting from the wrongful act or acts of another party (tort); to recovery property wrongfully taken by another party; for equitable distribution of property when joint ownership is being dissolved for whatever reason; etc., etc. Small claims must brought before the judge based on an established theory of law which permits the relief the claimant is requesting. The most common small claims are breach of written or verbal contract; an intentional or unintentional tort action (assault, battery, personal injury, property damage); disputed ownership of property; bounced checks; and failure to repay a loan or a promise to repay certain expenses such as shared utilities, charging on another party's credit card, etc. (verbal contracts).

It is not practical to hire an attorney to handle a small claim under $5,000 because filing fees and attorney fees will usually approach the value of the claim and there is no guarantee that the judge will award the relief sought. Therefore, many small claims are never pursued because the injured party cannot afford to hire an attorney and doesn't know how to file a small claim without an attorney.

Actually, filing a small claim and representing yourself is very simple because the court is informal and all the complex rules of evidence and procedural rules are not applicable in Small Claims Court. However, filing a small claim is not as it appears on "Judge Judy," or "Judge Joe Brown" TV shows where everything seems to revolve around the judge rather than the parties. The judge may informally question the parties in search of the truth but it is up to the parties to present a valid claim and to organize their evidence and testimony. A small claims judge is quick to dismiss a claim where no hard evidence or believable testimony is offered by the complainant.

The party filing the claim in Small Claims Court is called the "Plaintiff" and the party against whom the claim is filed is called the "Defendant." The court officer who assists the judge and calls the case to the bench is called the "Bailiff." If the court hearing is being recorded, it is usually being done by tape recording so there generally is no "Court Reporter." The decision by the judge is final and not subject to the appellate process. The judge will demand respect for the court, for the judge, and for the opposing party. The judge should always be addressed as "Your Honor" not "Judge" or "Sir" or anything else.

Before actually drafting your small claims petition to the court, it is prudent to first consider the nature of your claim (what legal theory of recovery you are relying upon?). Is your claim covered by contract law, property recovery law, equitable distribution of jointly owned property prior to dissolving of the joint relationship, default on a promise to repay (verbal contract), some type of tort (wrongful act), bounced check, or some other legal basis for recovery? Then consider whether you have any written agreement or other document which verifies your claim. What other documentation do you have to establish the cash value of your claim? Who do you know who can testify before the judge to back up your claim? Was this person an eye witness to the happenings or events that established your claim? Did the person just overhear the verbal contract or commitment establishing your claim? Is this person willing to testify before the judge? Seldom will your word against another party's word be sufficient for a judgment in your favor unless it is patently obvious to the judge that the opposing party is lying about the facts and circumstances surrounding your claim.

The next consideration is how to properly draft and submit your claim to the Small Claims Court clerk's office along with the required filing fee (again, call the court clerk to determine the amount of the filing fee). Following is a sample draft format that will be sufficient in virtually every Small Claims Court:

In the (name of court) for the (name of county), (name of state)

(name of plaintiff), Plaintiff,

v.

(name of defendant), Defendant.

Case number_____ (enter if

known)

PLAINTIFF'S CLAIM AGAINST DEFENDANT(S) FOR (DESCRIBE TYPE OF COMPLAINT)

Comes now Plaintiff (enter name) and with respect to the above captioned complaint states to the court:

1. Defendant resides in (county), (state) at (address); and Plaintiff resides in (county), (state), at (address). The events giving rise to this cause of action occurred in (county), (state). Because Defendant resides in said (county), and therefore can be found in said (county), jurisdiction and venue is

proper in the (name of court) for the county of (name of county).

2. (briefly describe without unnecessary and extraneous details the facts and circumstances giving rise to your claim. Description should be limited to fewest words possible but yet plainly state the facts and circumstances constituting your claim).

3. (state how the facts and circumstances stated in paragraphs (1) and (2) above caused physical injury or financial loss to you and how such physical injury or financial loss was calculated or

estimated).

WHEREFORE, Plaintiff respectfully prays the Court to (state what ruling you want from the Court); and for such further relief as the Court deems just and proper.

Respectfully submitted,

(signature of Plaintiff)

Printed name
address
telephone number
email (if any)

Make copies of all documents to be entered into evidence and attach originals to your petition before filing it with the small claims court clerk.

Attachments to Petition:

(describe attachments)

Certificate of Service

The undersigned hereby certifies that a true and complete copy of the foregoing complaint was served upon Defendant by (state how Defendant was officially served). Check with clerk of the court to ascertain your options for service upon Defendant).

_____
(signature of Plaintiff)

The court clerk will notify you what date and time to appear in court. Take a copy of your complaint to court with you. Travel to court early to make sure you arrive on time. When the court Bailiff calls your case, walk immediately to the front of judge's bench and identify yourself. The Defendant should do likewise.

It is customary for Plaintiff to address the court first followed by Defendant's statements in opposition. When the judge gives the nod or tells you to proceed, simply read or paraphrase from your copy of your complaint. When you state something for which you have documentary evidence, describe it to the judge. The bailiff will take the document and hand to the judge. Answer the judge's questions, if any. Then, proceed to finish your opening statement. If you have a witness, inform the judge and the judge will call and question the witness. If you have more than one witness, inform the judge and the judge will call and question the additional witness or witnesses. Do not interrupt the judge during the questioning of your witness or witnesses.

    When the judge signals the Defendant to offer statements in opposition, do not interrupt the Defendant or the judge. You will have a chance to rebut the Defendant's statements in opposition to your complaint. Follow the judge's lead in connection with additional opportunities to rebut statements by Defendant.

After listening to you and Defendant(s) and evaluating evidence and witness testimony submitted by you and Defendant(s), the judge will decide the case (usually after a short recess) the same day. The judge will give each party a copy of the judgment rendered or the court clerk will mail a copy to each party.

Chapter Seven

Filing For A Legal Name Change

LEGALLY CHANGING YOUR NAME

You do not need the services of an attorney to legally change your name. It is a simple and routine legal process that does not involve an adversarial court proceeding or naming an adverse party and serving notice on any defendant. To obtain a court approved name change, a simple petition must be presented to the appropriate local court where the judge will issue an order officially approving your name change.

The main requirement for obtaining a court sanctioned name change is that the petitioner must state under oath that the requested name change is not for the purpose of committing a crime or interfering with the rights of others, or for any other fraudulent or illegal purpose, or to hide from creditors. You probably cannot get court approval to change your name to Barack Obama, or Glen Beck or Sarah Palin in order to take advantage of another individual's celebrity status.

To legally change your name, first call the Circuit Clerk's office for the county in which you reside and ascertain which local court you must petition for a name change. Then contact the clerk's office for that specific court and inquire concerning the court's address, the required filing fee and whether the clerk's office provides an official petition form for a name change. If the court has adopted an official petition form, have the clerk's office mail the form to you. Fill out the form, sign and date it before a notary public and mail it back to the clerk's office along with the required filing fee.

If the court you must petition has not adopted an official petition form, draft your petition, sign and date it before a notary public and mail to the court clerk's office along with the required filing fee. Following is a sample petition for an official name change:

IN THE ASSOCIATE CIRCUIT COURT FOR MORGAN COUNTY, MISSOURI

Case Number _____

PETITION FOR LEGAL CHANGE OF NAME

Sally Ann Jones, Petitioner

    Comes now Petitioner Sally Ann Jones and petitions the above captioned Court under oath, as evidenced by the below signed Notary Public, to approve and order the official name change of Petitioner from Sally Ann Jones to Mary Sue Smith. Petitioner certifies to the Court that the requested name change is not for the purpose of concealing a crime, or for interfering with the rights of others, or for any fraudulent or illegal purpose.

    WHEREFORE, Petitioner prays this Honorable Court to approve and order Petitioner's name changed from Sally Ann Jones to Mary Sue Smith.

Respectfully submitted,

Sally Ann Jones, Petitioner
31578 Calvary Drive
Rocky Mount, Missouri 65072
(573) 494-3616
email: saj9230@gmail.com

NOTARY PUBLIC

County of Morgan   )
State of Missouri   )s.s.

On this 27th day of August, 2010, before me personally appeared Sally Ann Jones who, after being officially identified by me and duly sworn, stated to me that she is the individual who prepared and executed the forgoing petition for a court approved name change from Sally Ann Jones to Mary Sue Smith.

_____

Notary Public

Seal

August 27, 2010

My Commission expires December 31, 2013.

    Of course, the name of the court; the name of the Petitioner; all dates, addresses, county and state; and the Notary identification must conform to the actual situation of Petitioner and the desired new name.

For a properly drafted petition sworn to before a notary public, an actual court hearing may not be necessary in some court jurisdictions. The judge may just sign an order to be mailed to you by the court clerk.

If an actual hearing is required, the court clerk will notify you of the scheduled hearing date. Simply attend the hearing and identify yourself to the judge when the

Court Bailiff calls your case number assigned by the court clerk. Answer any questions addressed to you by the judge after being officially sworn in. The hearing will not last more than five minutes or so after your case is called.

Check list for notice to be given of name change:

Post office

Motor Vehicles Administration

Social Security Administration

Any will, estate planning document, and any trust entity

Driver's license

U.S. Passport

Friends and family

Library,

Employers

Doctors and Pharmacists

Banks and other financial institutions serving you

Creditor and debtors

Telephone and utility companies

Department of Vital Statistics

Birth certificate

Municipal, state and federal taxing authorities

Voter registration

Miscellaneous others who need to know of your name change

For most of the above notifications, it is best to furnish a copy of the court order approving your name change.

www.ingramcontent.com/pod-product-compliance
Lightning Source LLC
Chambersburg PA
CBHW061511180526
45171CB00001B/134